Missing from the
Mueller Report

Leo Goldstein

Dedicated to all targets of the modern witch hunts

Copyright

© 2019 SHFi (Science for Humans and Freedom Institute) / Leo Goldstein

All Rights Reserved. For permissions and other copyright related questions, please email contact@defyccc.com

Edition 1.14

March 2019

ISBN (paperback): 978-1-7338922-1-6

"... an attempted coup by Comey and his crowd"

"Little did I know that it appears that they were all in it together. I mean Rosenstein, Comey, Mueller, McCabe, the whole crowd and they were out to get this president no matter what. I don't think they sincerely believed anything about Russia. ... **I mean it's a coup. That's what it is an attempted coup by Comey and his crowd. And the evidence is all over there.**"

John Dowd, Trump's former attorney[1]

Contents

Copyright 3
"... an attempted coup by Comey and his crowd" 4
Contents 5
Introduction 6
Robert Mueller's Agendas 8
    Mueller, a Partner in WilmerHale 8
    130k Yuans 13
    Other Misadventures and Conflicts of Interest 17
There was No Russian Interference 26
    The Weightless "Intelligence Community Assessment" 26
    The FBI/DHS Report GRIZZLY STEPPE Was Junk 30
    Imaginary Social Media Component of Imaginary Russian Interference 32
    "Russian Activities" in 2016 Elections Were anti-Trump 34
    Climate of Fear in Cyber-Security 38
Final Remarks 43
Appendix ROBERT MUELLER: UNMASKED, by Louie Gohmert (R-TX) 44
Acknowledgments 54
About the Author 54
Endnotes and References 55

Introduction

Circumstances surrounding the appointment of Special Counsel Robert Mueller are suspect at best. A Special Counsel is appointed only to investigate a specific crime, and only if the DOJ has a conflict of interest[2]. In other words, a Special Counsel is appointed to investigate something in the DOJ, rather than the other way around. Rod Rosenstein made Robert Mueller a Special Counsel in violation of both requirements[3].

The allegations of Russian interference against Hillary Clinton were conceived by the DNC and the Hillary campaign for election purposes and were controverted by Donald Trump. Nevertheless, the Special Counsel assumed they were incontrovertible fact. It also failed to specify what crime the Special Counsel was supposed to investigate. Robert Mueller had more conflicts of interest than almost any lawyer in the country. He was friends with James Comey, John Brennan, and many other perpetrators of Spygate. Even more of his disqualifying conduct is discussed in this book.

In short, the appointment of the Special Counsel was part of a coup, started by holdovers from the Obama administration with encouragement and support from foreign governments and supranational bodies, including the European Commission.

The news reports suggest that McCabe, Comey, and a few others in the FBI imagined themselves kingmakers, with an authority to suspect and investigate the President, who had been duly elected and confirmed by Congress! The Constitution doesn't vest the FBI with such authority, even if there are real grounds for suspicion that the President is a "Russian asset" – such as when President Obama and Secretary Clinton approved the sale of Uranium One and the transfer of advanced dual purpose technologies (via Skolkovo) to the Russian Federation. Not to mention that all the while the Clintons and the Clinton Foundation cashed hefty checks from Russia[4]. But the real reason behind the DOJ's conduct was not "suspicion" but the dynamics of a coup. Once the coup attempt started and became public, it could not be stopped. Cheered by the media and celebrities, the coup has been escalating. Appointing the Special Counsel with a mandate to weaken the President in order to create conditions for his overthrow was a logical next step in their attempt.

Robert Mueller's Agendas

What's wrong with Robert Mueller? He was registered as a Republican two decades ago, but that doesn't mean anything now. He became known for maliciously prosecuting Republicans – see the Appendix. He served in the Obama administration for two years. He was not known as a partisan Democrat, possibly because he didn't advertise his political views. On many occasions, he has abused his prosecutorial powers to get his targets, and not limited to Republicans. He has shown a habit of deciding the outcome of an investigation first, and then using and abusing all means to convict the target, ignoring evidence pointing in other directions. Still, when he was appointed as a Special Counsel, nobody expected such malicious behavior.

Mueller, a Partner in WilmerHale

In 2014, soon after his retirement from the FBI, Robert Mueller joined the law firm WilmerHale in Washington. There he received an annual compensation of about $3.5M – a common way in which high level public officers later capitalize on their contacts and insider's access. 84% of the WilmerHale political contributions went to Democrats[5] in the 2012 election campaign. In the 2016 elections, WilmerHale contributed $331,038 to Hillary Clinton[6] and only $428 to Donald Trump. Yes, the ratio is 773:1. Seems one-sided, doesn't it? Somebody in WilmerHale might have thought they made a wrong bet. And it is hard to believe that partner Robert Mueller was not affected by the mood in the company. WilmerHale also has a large office in Beijing, the only WilmerHale office outside of the US and the EU[7]. More importantly,

WilmerHale is a legal representative and super-lobbyist for China[8]. WilmerHale achieved the most spectacular trade benefits for China. This is how the firm brags[9] about that (emphasis is mine here and throughout the remainder of the book):

With respect to China, our team includes the chief US architect and negotiator of China's entry into the WTO and one of the leading regulatory lawyers in Beijing (and a member of the Board of Governors of the American Chamber of Commerce—People's Republic of China). ...

In advising on trade policy and trade negotiations, we have helped develop or shape key trade initiatives and legislation both in and outside government, including Congress' landmark grant of Permanent Normal Trade Relations to China; negotiating priorities in the Trans-Pacific Partnership free trade agreement negotiations; *congressional implementation of various US free trade agreements; and trade-related provisions in internet, patent and drug importation legislation.*

These benefits to China are directly threatened by President Trump. WilmerHale partners, including Robert Mueller, have a direct interest in undermining or even impeaching him. Even if impeachment doesn't succeed, weakening Trump benefits China in the trade talks.

WilmerHale has a lot of other China-linked interests. It represents Chinese firms in the US and non-Chinese firms in China. It acknowledges close relationships with the Chinese government[10]:

The China team provides critical policy, regulatory and government relations advice that complements our clients' commercial objectives. We have represented clients across a broad range of industries in all aspects of their business dealings across China... Among the China practice's recent triumphs on behalf of its clients are the execution of copyright cooperation agreements for the publication of **local editions of several of the world's leading magazines; assistance in securing approvals for several of the largest and most novel foreign investments in China; favorable outcomes for Chinese producers in anti-dumping investigations in the United States; and successful litigations and investigations of intellectual property infringements.** *With the depth and breadth of our US and European offices,* **we have also advised Chinese entities** *on their outbound commercial and trade relations, particularly in obtaining regulatory approvals, structuring transactions and* **defending against trade actions***.*

And more:

To assist clients with these challenges and opportunities, our China Trade Practice offers a unique combination of services bringing together prominent policy, regulatory and **government relations capabilities in China** *with premier in-country business and transactions experience.*

Our commitment to the China market, its Fortune 100 and major multinational clientele doing business in or exporting to China, and Chinese entities doing business abroad is deep and growing. The firm's establishment of a Beijing office demonstrates this commitment. ...

The team possesses ... strong relationships with political, private sector, media and opinion leaders throughout China and East Asia as a whole. The China team includes professionals who have operated at the highest levels of the US Executive Branch ...

The unsurpassed combination of talents of the firm's China team, supported by the depth and breadth of our United States and European offices, allows the firm to marshal superior resources on behalf of our clients.[11]

WilmerHale is a leading, full-service international law firm with lawyers located throughout the United States, Europe and Asia. Our lawyers work at the intersection of government, technology and business ... [12]

In assisting companies in unfair trade investigations, we obtained the lowest duty rate among the Big Three auto companies in an antidumping and countervailing duty case brought by China; ... **in the biggest US anti dumping case against China to date, our clients were the only Chinese producers that were found to be not subject to duties.[13]**

Not surprisingly, WilmerHale also does pro bono work for "the Resistance". For example, it sued the US to force the military to accept individuals suffering from gender identity disorder[14] (such as Bradley/Chelsea Manning), and it sued Texas to enable voting fraud[15]:

For several years, along with the NAACP Legal Defense and Educational Fund, represented a single plaintiff challenging Texas' unduly restrictive and racially discriminatory voter identification requirements.

In August 2017, filed suit on behalf of five Jane Doe plaintiffs seeking to declare that the US president's directive to categorically exclude transgender people from military service is unconstitutional and to enjoin its enforcement.

Remember banning Pepe the Frog from social media? WilmerHale is behind that, too:

On behalf of the creator of Pepe the Frog, enforced intellectual property rights to shut down distribution of a controversial children's book that featured a character named Pepe the Frog...

Contrary to the practice of most law firms concerned about potential conflicts of interest, WilmerHale has an alumni network and is *"committed to maintaining close ties with"* its former lawyers[16]. Whether Robert Mueller is considered an alum or a current partner on a Special Assignment, he immediately placed three of his WilmerHale partners[17] on his Special Team: Jeannie Rhee, who formerly represented a top Obama aide and the Clinton Foundation; James Quarles, the head of the WilmerHale DC office, and thus probably the point man for the Chinese government; and Aaron Zebley. He also stuffed his team with "angry Democrats," but this is out of the book's scope.

Thus, Mueller's witch hunt undermines the US not only in its negotiations with China, but also in our confrontation with North Korea. Mueller weakens the executive branch, and the US is forced to negotiate with North Korea from this position of weakness. The same applies to relations with Iran.

130k Yuans

On March 7, 2017, Robert Mueller delivered a 45-minute presentation titled *The Growing Cyber Security Threat* at a conference co-hosted by International Data Group (IDG), in which he articulated and publicly committed himself to the DNC conspiracy theory that "Russia had hacked the democracy". Mueller's presentation was quoted as follows:

"What the Russians are doing is a huge threat," said Mueller, adding that such cyberthreats to democracy are, in a sense, "more devastating than terrorist attacks — the one-offs that you currently have in the United States."[18] (Forbes)

In terms of the top cybersecurity threats the U.S. government faces today, Mueller laid out five threat vectors: 1) Protecting democracy from Russian hackers and others that want to undercut democracy ...[19] (FedTechMag)

Mueller had no grounds for those remarks at that time. Even the so-called *Intelligence Community Assessment* from Jan 6, 2017, didn't go that far, and Mueller should have known that that report had been cooked within four weeks under the supervision of Obama political appointees and should be treated as at least suspicious, if not an outright political hatchet job. If he had looked around, he would have found that the Assessment had been refuted within a few days of its publication. For example, Fox News published a long piece by former CIA analyst Fred Fleitz *"Was Friday's declassified report claiming Russian hacking of the 2016 election rigged?"*[20], referring to the interview with the former House Intelligence Committee Chairman Pete Hoekstra[21]. Hoekstra pointed to the fact that the "assessment" had been issued by only three intelligence agencies instead of the claimed 17 ones, and the most important agencies – DIA and DHS – were missing. Fred Fleitz was direct in saying, *"I also suspect the entire purpose of this report and its timing was to provide President Obama with a supposedly objective intelligence report on Russian interference in the 2016 election that the president could release before he left office to undermine the legitimacy of Trump's election."* The timing of the release and the way in which it had been shopped around by James Clapper suggest that the ambitions of its authors were much bigger – to block certification of the Presidential election by Congress! After the successful certification and inauguration of President Trump, the "Russian interference" narrative started dying until Mueller breathed new life into it. For all that, Mueller was paid $24,000 and possibly prospects for future business opportunities.

The timing of Mueller's speech is important. Jeff Sessions recused himself from supervising the mislabeled "Russian investigation" on March 2, 2017. The Democrats were not satisfied and demanded the appointment of a special counsel. They have strong cards – Rod Rosenstein was already nominated as Deputy Attorney General, but Senate confirmation hearings hadn't started. The Democrats could reasonably expect that DAG would give them "special counsel on demand". Robert Mueller delivered his presentation on March 7th, thereby passing an audition for the role of the special counsel. I have no information whether he knew that or not and assume he didn't. In the following Rosenstein confirmation hearings, Senate Democrats showed that they wanted Rosenstein to appoint a special counsel to continue the "Russian investigation," and they were probably satisfied. Rosenstein was sworn in on April 26th. On May 9th, he wrote a memo recommending firing James Comey, and President Trump fired Comey[22]. Over the course of the following week, McCabe and Rosenstein discussed removing Trump from office. "Wearing a wire" and purporting to invoke the 25th Amendment were some ideas that became public. Finally, on May 17th, Rosenstein created the Special Counsel and appointed Robert Mueller. Mueller's commitment to the "Russian election hacking" conspiracy theory was likely helpful.

At the time of Mueller's speech, IDG was owned by China Oceanwide Holdings Group, which is owned by a top official in the Chinese government and the Communist Party of China. Yes, at least some of the top officials in the Communist Party of China are billionaires. Curiously, Oceanwide announced acquisition of the IDG[23] on January 19, 2017 – the last day of the Obama administration. A closer look at the China Oceanwide structure and operation of the IDG suggests that IDG was indeed acquired by China to serve as a vehicle for espionage and/or political influence.

Mueller also lied about this transaction on his financial disclosure (*OGE Form 278e*)[24], concealing that he received money from a Chinese intelligence front. This is the copy of the entry:

| 6.7 | CDW/IDG Enterprise (Washington, DC) - 3/7/2017 | N/A | Honorarium | $24,900 |

Instead of International Data Group, Mueller listed non-existent CDW/IDG Enterprise. IDG Enterprise is an unrelated small consultancy located in Massachusetts. Mueller also refused to disclose other conflicts of interest, and DOJ "career employees" granted him a conflict-of-interest waiver[25].

The only reason for Mueller to suspect Trump of colluding with Russia might be projection. Otherwise, a reasonable conclusion would be that this transaction and his related business at WilmerHale merely influenced his decision-making. But Mueller's other conflicts of interest deserve consideration as well.

IDG and China Oceanwide

The CDW/IDG conference has web presence on cio.com, a website of IDG Communications, Inc., a subsidiary of IDG[26]. IDG owner China Oceanwide Holdings Group[27] is headed by Mr. Lu Zhiqiang, a high-level official of the government and the Communist Party of China. Its website says:

China Oceanwide Holdings Group was founded in 1985 by Mr. Lu Zhiqiang, the founder, legal representative, **Communist Party secretary**, *chairman and president of the group. ...*

Mr. Lu Zhiqiang is the founder, legal representative, **Communist Party secretary**, *chairman of the Group, who also serves as* **a member of the standing committee of the 12th Chinese People's Political Consultative Conference, vice president of the China Chamber of Commerce**, *deputy chairman of the Oceanwide Foundation, deputy chairman of the China Foundation for Guangcai Program, vice chairman of the Chinese Art and Literature Foundation, and deputy chairman of China Minsheng Bank ...*

Mr. Lu Zhiqiang officially appointed himself the Chairman of the IDG Board[28] on March 29, 2017 – six weeks before Mueller became Special Counsel. IDG owns many information technology publications and venues, including security-focused CIO.com and csoonline.com. I wonder when anybody will start to care about non-friendly foreign ownership, financing, and advertising in the US media?

Other Misadventures and Conflicts of Interest

In 2013, Robert Mueller spent some time "lecturing" about cyber-security at Stanford University. Stanford University is in the heart of Silicon Valley. Mueller was an experienced prosecutor and FBI director, but he knew next to nothing about anything cyber. Such academic practice of hiring former government officials smacks of corruption. Most likely, during his time in Silicon Valley, Mueller built important connections with Big Tech and picked up leftist views. Mueller represented multiple Silicon Valley companies as a WilmerHale partner, including Facebook and Apple. InfoWars, Alex Jones' channel, regularly and relentlessly criticized the conduct of the Special Counsel. When Special Counsel Mueller wanted to break down former InfoWars editor Dr. Jerome Corsi and contributor Roger Stone, his former WilmerHale clients (Facebook and Apple), together with other *Masters of the Universe,* banned InfoWars from their platforms **simultaneously – within hours of each other**[29]!

Google, Facebook, Apple, and Spotify banned InfoWars on August 6, 2018. Mueller subpoenaed Dr. Corsi exactly 30 days later[30]. Twitter permanently banned InfoWars the next day on September 6th. Google YouTube banned The Alex Jones Channel[31], which had nearly 2.5 million subscribers. This appears a coordination between the Mueller team and the *Masters of the Universe* to prevent Roger Stone and Dr. Corsi from communicating their ordeals to the public. Most likely, the coordination between Mueller's team and the *Masters of the Universe* happened indirectly through some group affiliated with the Democratic Party, such as the Center for American Progress (CAP): somebody on Mueller's team and somebody affiliated with CAP talked about the investigation, and then CAP issued demands to the *Masters of the Universe*, which they quickly fulfilled.

Mueller Represented Facebook and Apple

In February 2018, Robert Mueller made a pointless indictment[32] of Russian citizens and corporations for Facebook posts alleged to have sown division and interfered with the 2016 elections (*USA v. Internet Research Agency et al*). Indictment of Russian citizens who live in Russia and don't intend to travel to the US or countries that would cooperate with the US is useless. Indictment of Russian corporations without assets or interests in the US is worse than useless. Foreign corporations can defend themselves in the US courts through US attorneys, with many of the same rights that defendants enjoy in the criminal proceedings, without subjecting themselves to de-facto US jurisdiction. That includes discovery of the materials in the prosecutor's file. One of the indicted Russian corporations availed itself of such an option. Some materials from the Special Counsel file, which is closed to the public, have been transferred to the corporation's lawyers. Then Mueller started crying that altered copies of these materials have been released on the internet[33]. Notice that Mueller's team wants to remove President Trump from office. In this light, it is not clear whether the decision to indict Russian corporations was incompetent (as thought by Andrew McCarthy of the *National Review*) or diabolical.

If individuals and corporations, representing or controlled by the Russian government, made election interference posts "on Facebook", they contracted with Facebook. In this case, they also paid Facebook about $50k prior to the election. Thus, Facebook aided and enabled foreign election interference. Russian citizens and corporations are beyond reach and beyond control. But Facebook is here. Facebook is the only entity that can be held accountable for the alleged misconduct. No, the deal that Facebook and Twitter made with Congressional Democrats – to suppress conservative voices and to call some of them Russian trolls or even bots[34] – doesn't release them from liability. The famous Section 230 might shield Facebook from responsibility for the content of the posts, but not for making a contract or an agreement with a foreign government, its instrumentality, or even a private entity, when such contract or agreement enables them to interfere in the US elections. Why didn't Mueller indict Facebook? Para 2 of the indictment should have looked like this:

Defendant INTERNET RESEARCH AGENCY LLC ("ORGANIZATION") is a Russian organization engaged in operations to interfere with elections and political processes. Defendants MIKHAIL IVANOVICH BYSTROV, ... **and FACEBOOK LLC** [added – LG] *worked in various capacities to carry out Defendant ORGANIZATION's interference operations targeting the United States. From in or around 2014 to the present, Defendants knowingly and intentionally conspired with each other (and with persons known and unknown to the Grand Jury) ... the purpose of interfering with the U.S. political and electoral processes, including the presidential election of 2016.*

But Facebook was among the largest clients that Mueller represented as a WilmerHale partner (one of the ten clients listed in the disclosure). Mueller also holds a small amount of Facebook stock[35].

CrowdStrike Link

One of the biggest scandals of Spygate is the FBI's failure to inspect the DNC network to determine the source of its hack(s). Instead, the FBI completely relied on the information received from CrowdStrike, the DNC contractor. Ostensibly, investigating Hillary's bathroom email server left Comey and his subordinates in the FBI much too scared, so they decided to stay away from the DNC computers and to take all computer-related information from the DNC as truth.

When the DNC network was hacked in September 2015 – June 2016 and the hackers got access to troves of data that likely included classified national security information, the DNC refused to give the FBI access to its network and then it destroyed the evidence. The DNC called in CrowdStrike, a shady cybersecurity firm with ties to the Democratic Party and Obama's FBI, to investigate and/or cover up the incident. Why hasn't Mueller investigated CrowdStrike, the DNC cybersecurity contractor and likely the DNC's accomplice in the evidence destruction?

One of CrowdStrike's owners and top officers is Shawn Henry, Mueller's protégé and executive assistant director in the FBI who remained in contact with Mueller after moving to CrowdStrike[36]. Shawn Henry is also an NBC News consultant. That helps to sync fake news with a fake investigation, doesn't it? CrowdStrike general counsel Steve Chabinsky is another Mueller assistant director.

CrowdStrike is the original source of all the alleged evidence[37] behind the claim that the DNC data had been stolen and leaked by the Russian government. Other companies and, apparently, intelligence services entirely relied on the data from CrowdStrike and significantly relied on the attribution by CrowdStrike. Shawn Henry and Dmitri Alperovitch of Crowdstrike were invited, but they refused[38] to testify before the House Intel Committee.

Has Mueller Violated the Logan Act?

The names of some of the 12 alleged GRU officers uselessly indicted by Robert Mueller on July 13, 2018 – for the sole purpose of sabotaging President Trump before the US-Russia summit – are a Russian military secret. They have probably been obtained by covert means. Thus, Mueller likely compromised the CIA methods and sources used to obtain these names. This might be a violation of *18 U.S. Code § 798* (Disclosure of classified information) and/or *50 U.S. Code § 3121* (Protection of identities of certain United States undercover intelligence officers, agents, informants, and sources), each carrying a penalty of up to 10 years in prison.

Even worse, by making and publishing that indictment, Mueller sent Putin a written message, saying that the US presidency was weak, and Russia could harden its positions in multiple disputes with the US. This was a clear violation of the Logan Act, as amended in 1994.

Skolkovo: Mueller, Hillary, and the Masters of the Universe – OMG!

For those who don't know yet, the term *Masters of the Universe* refers to Google, Facebook, Twitter, Microsoft, Apple, and maybe a couple other Big Tech companies that imagined they can decide what we are allowed to read, watch, and say. I saw this term applied to them in Breitbart first.

Remember how Hillary supported Skolkovo[39], the technological espionage project of Russia? From the Skolkovo project website (2015):

The innovative development of nuclear technologies is an essential condition for consolidating (and in some areas, achieving) a position of global technological leadership and maintaining Russia's defense capability.[40]

Developing the space sector ... boosting living standards while helping to ensure national security [41]

Intel and Facebook heavily contributed to Skolkovo when Robert Mueller was their attorney. Intel and Microsoft were Skolkovo Foundation Partners[42]. Google Chairman Eric Schmidt became a Skolkovo board member. Google is also one of the biggest investors in CrowdStrike. In Skolkovo, Google and Facebook aided the Russian Federation with the development of facial recognition and computer vision systems[43] that have military and intelligence applications. They might have even tested these systems in the US. The results are quite impressive[44]. Twitter was there, too.

From the *National Review*: *Russian Collusion, Clinton $tyle*[45] and *How the Clintons Sold Out U.S. National Interests to the Putin Regime*[46]:

Hillary pushed Skolkovo, 'a high-tech corridor in Russia modeled after our own Silicon Valley,' as she explained in Moscow in October 2009. Her State Department colleagues encouraged 22 top American venture capitalists to tour Skolkovo in May 2010. State [Department] convinced Cisco, Google, and Intel, among others, to open shop in Skolkovo. By 2012, 28 'Key Partners' from the U.S., Europe, and Russia supported this project.

17 out of the 28 were also donors to the Clinton Foundation.

But the U.S. Army Foreign Military Studies Program warned in 2013: 'Skolkovo is arguably an overt alternative to clandestine industrial espionage.'

*Hillary captured its essence in March 2010 when she told former Soviet propagandist Vladimir Pozner on First Channel TV: **'Our goal is to help strengthen Russia.'*** [47]

Misc.

Notice that persons indicted by Mueller can be divided into two distinct, not intersecting groups, totally unconnected to each other[48]:

>a) Russian persons located in Russia and out of reach of the US courts, or

b) Americans close to Trump with no substantial connections to Russia.

Mueller has never been an investigator, only a prosecutor and a lawyer. Hardly anybody on the top level of his team has ever been an investigator. In 2014, Mueller admitted on camera: *"I became a prosecutor because I liked putting people in jail."* Representative Louie Gohmert (R-TX) has recently published a report **Robert Mueller: UNMASKED**[49]. See excerpts and my comments in the Appendix.

There was No Russian Interference

Not only was there no Trump-Russia collusion, but not even was there any Russian interference in favor of Trump. The Podesta and DNC leaks came from insider(s) and independent hacker(s) – probably disgruntled Bernie supporters. Craig Murray, former British Ambassador to Uzbekistan, acknowledged[50] on December 14th, 2016 that he had received DNC documents from a DNC insider and transferred them to WikiLeaks. Craig Murray is not a Trump supporter.

WikiLeaks might have received the DNC documents from multiple sources, including hackers not affiliated with the Russian state. On the other hand, there is no sufficient evidence to suggest that Seth Rich was involved. Other hackers, leakers, or persons with knowledge of what transpired might have surfaced by now, if Mueller's investigation were not conducted as a witch hunt. Mueller persecutes and attempts to manufacture charges against everybody potentially knowledgeable of the DNC/DCCC/Podesta data leak circumstances, so nobody comes forward.

It can be shown by technical indicators that the attribution of the DNC leaks to the Russian state was incorrect, but that is beyond the scope of this book.

The Weightless "Intelligence Community Assessment"

An article in *The New Yorker*[51], promoting the "Russian interference" conspiracy theory, referred to the first week of December 2016 as the time "***when Obama was intent***

on an orderly transfer of power." The real meaning of this phrase is that Obama had failed to orderly transfer power to the elected administration – the first time in more than 200 years! On December 9th, *Washington Post* published[52] a putative leak, falsely alleging that "*Intelligence agencies have identified individuals with connections to the Russian government who provided WikiLeaks with thousands of hacked emails from the Democratic National Committee and others*" and other lies. Notice that Mueller has failed to identify such individuals more than two years later. The article also incorrectly claimed "*that's the consensus view*" of the Intelligence Community. On the same day, Obama ordered a full review of the alleged Russian hacking, to be led by James Clapper, and delivered before January 20th. But the "full review" was completed much faster – on January 5th. Miraculously, it then took only one day to prepare an unclassified version of it! Of course, miracles don't happen. Brennan and Clapper made a forgery and released it the morning of January 6th to block the certification of the Presidential election by Congress!

Note that the Mueller investigation has been going on for almost two years – more than twenty times longer than the preparation of the *Intelligence Community Assessment*[53], the only official document to which all claims of Russian election interference are sourced. Mueller has not found any validation of that assessment. This *Assessment* has been thoroughly refuted. First, it wasn't what the MSM purported it to be:

- It was not an *Intelligence Community Coordinated Assessment*, but a hatchet job by Brennan, Clapper, and a handful of their accomplices[54].
- It was not a consensus product of 17 intelligence agencies but of a few individuals from the CIA, FBI, and NSA who were provided cherry-picked information. The most important data, such as firewall logs and forensic images of DNC computers from April-May 2016, was not even collected.
- Brennan and Clapper repeatedly lied about this process.

All the lines of "proof" in the *Assessment* have been refuted:

- The allegation that RT (Russia Today TV) aided Trump against Hillary is false; on the contrary, RT supported Democrats against Republicans and Hillary against Trump. Among Democrats, RT did prefer Bernie to Hillary.
- The allegation that the IRA (a "troll farm" in Russia) media buys were directed by the Kremlin, or any single entity, is shown to be wrong. By the way, IRA bought ads in rubles. Do Brennan, Clapper, Mueller et al think that Russian intelligence is *that stupid*?
- The assessment was based on the junk FBI/DHS Report GRIZZLY STEPPE.
- The "classified evidence" in the Assessment likely comprises:
    - CrowdStrike[55] forgeries.

- A chain of misattributions by CrowdStrike and FireEye/Mandiant.
- Disinformation from German BfV and, possibly, some other Western European governments that have developed a habit of blaming the Russian government not only for cyber incidents but for public dissatisfaction with their policies.
- A summary of the infamous "Steele dossier". Note that the Steele dossier was an obvious hoax that was ordered, funded, and disseminated by the DNC. The classified summary of it might have had the effect of whitewashing the Steele dossier and giving it the appearance of a legitimate intelligence report. The Steele dossier was entirely refuted. Steve McIntyre[56] noted in Oct 2017: *"The writer of the Steele dossier incorporated numerous public details which give the memoranda more weight to a credulous reader than they deserve. **AFAIK, anything in the dossier that is true was known publicly; and anything in the dossier that was not drawn from public sources and which can be crosschecked (e.g. Michael Cohen in Prague) is false.**"* And it is proven to be so.

Finally, the authors of the assessment ignored the fact that the DNC was refusing to cooperate[57] with the FBI from September 2015 until August 2016, by which time it had already destroyed all the evidence.

The hoax has been so successful partly because Big Tech (especially Google, Facebook, Twitter, Microsoft, and Apple) has sided with the Democratic Party, silenced cyber security experts[58], repeatedly lied to Congress, and refused to collaborate with the Trump administration.

The FBI/DHS Report GRIZZLY STEPPE Was Junk

The *GRIZZLY STEPPE – Russian Malicious Cyber Activity*[59] released jointly by the FBI and DHS on December 29, 2016, was an update to the *Joint Statement from DHS and ODNI on Election Security.* The latter was a pre-election propaganda piece, published by the Obama administration on October 7th to support the Democratic party narrative and to aid Hillary in the elections.

GRIZZLY STEPPE was so incompetent that even convinced partisans laughed it off. From *The Daily Beast,* January 7, 2017 [60]:

'At every level this report is a failure,' *says security researcher* **Robert M. Lee**. *'It didn't do what it set out to do, and it didn't provide useful data. They're handing out bad information to the industry when good information exists.'*

... the report is a gumbo of earnest security advice mixed with random information from a broad range of hacking activity. *One piece of well-known malware used by criminal hackers, the PAS webshell, is singled out for special attention, while the sophisticated Russian 'SeaDuke' code used in the DNC hack barely rates a mention. A full page of the report is dedicated to listing names that computer security companies have assigned* *to Russian malware and hacking groups over the years, information that nobody is asking for. ...*

Though the written report is confusing, it's the raw data released along with it that truly exasperates security professionals. *The department released 876 internet IP addresses it says is linked to Grizzly Steppe hacking, and urged network administrators everywhere to add the list to their networking monitoring. ...*

We had an extraordinary high amount of false positives on this dataset... Six of them were Yahoo e-mail servers.
...

It turns out that some, perhaps most, of the watchlisted addresses have a decidedly weak connection to the Kremlin, if any. **In addition to the Yahoo servers, about 44 percent of the addresses are exit nodes in the Tor anonymity network***, The Intercept's Micah Lee reported Wednesday. Tor is free software used primarily for anonymous web browsing. Russian hackers use Tor, but so do plenty of other people. ...*

The consequences of the over inclusive list became apparent last week, when a Vermont utility company, Burlington Electric Department, followed DHS's advice and added the addresses to its network monitoring setup. It got an alert within a day. The utility called the feds, and The Washington Post soon broke the distressing news that "Russian hackers penetrated [the] U.S. electricity grid through a utility in Vermont. ...

The story was wrong. Not only was the laptop in question isolated from the utility's control systems, **the IP address that triggered the alert wasn't dangerous after all***: It was one of the Yahoo servers on the DHS list, and the alert had been generated by a Burlington Electric employee checking email. The Post article was later corrected, but not before* **Vermont Senator Patrick Leahy issued a statement condemning the putative Russian attack.**

These false positives fed the media frenzy for months. The extreme incompetence of the report indicates that the heads of the FBI and DHS didn't use ordinary channels and procedures, but they hand-picked report writers based on individual or political loyalty.

Imaginary Social Media Component of Imaginary Russian Interference

The social media component of the alleged "Russian activities in the 2016 elections" was non-existent. The IRA, a.k.a. the "troll farm" in Russia, *allegedly* bought ads for about $100k; this is chump change and not even worthy of a government operation. Most of it was spent on Facebook, and most ads ran **AFTER the 2016 elections**. Much of the rest ran between June 2015 and May 2016, long before election day. There were no signs of anti-Hillary or pro-Trump bias. There were no links between IRA ad buys and RT. No evidence of involvement by the Russian government. No evidence that the ad buys were part of a coordinated campaign. On the contrary, the ads seem to be bought for different entities or even by individuals for fun, profit, and/or self-expression. 75% of all the ads were not targeted at specific states[61], and only 10% of the ads were targeted at swing states[62]. And political ads are not that effective in changing minds: *"Did anyone really listen to the ads? I think most of us tune them out almost immediately as political noise."*[63] But the "accounts linked to IRA" placed 3,000-3,500 ads, so it's always possible to cherry pick a few of them to support any wild claim.

Facebook refuted the allegations of the Russian interference[64] in September 2017, although they kept the misleading article title because of the political pressure:

An Update On Information Operations On Facebook

The vast majority of ads run by these accounts didn't specifically reference the US presidential election, voting or a particular candidate.

Attempts to interpret the purported IRA ads as election related, even without connection to Trump, led to ridiculous statements in the article like *We read every one of the 3,517 Facebook ads bought by Russians. Here's what we found* (USA Today, May 2018)[65]:

While some ads focused on topics as banal as business promotion or Pokémon, the company consistently promoted ads designed to inflame race-related tensions.

"These ads broadly sought to pit one American against another by exploiting faults in our society or race, ethnicity, sexual orientation and other deeply cynical thoughts," Schiff [D-CA] said in an interview with USA TODAY NETWORK.

This is exactly what Democrats have been doing since the 2016 election campaign.

"Russian Activities" in 2016 Elections Were anti-Trump

It's almost funny that the so-called *Intelligence Community Assessment* claimed that the Russian interference had been against Hillary and in favor of Trump, although most of the evidence in it demonstrated the opposite. RT agitated in favor of Hillary and the policies of the Democratic Party and against Trump and the policies of the Republican Party.

The Nation is Leftist. It is far from being pro-Trump. Nevertheless, it pointed out that RT was not 'pro-Trump'[66]. This is what it says on the subject, with links to the RT footage:

The problem with the claim that RT America is pro-Trump is that it is simply false. Many of the channel's biggest names were either ardently anti-Trump or highly skeptical of what a Trump presidency might mean for America. ...

Chris Hedges, a Pulitzer Prize–winning journalist and former Middle East bureau chief for The New York Times and host of the show On Contact, had a consistent anti-Trump outlook. Hedges called Trump "woefully unprepared"[67] for the presidency and said his election could mean the creation of a "draconian police state." ...

Stalwart liberal Thom Hartmann, who hosts The Big Picture, has aired programs with names like: Dictator Trump Threatens Free Speech,[68] Why Trump's Cabinet Is a

Basket of Deplorables,[69] How Trump Could Bring on the Crash of 2016,[70] Does Trump Mean the End of the Internet as We Know It?,[71] Why Trump's Win Is a Koch Coup Against Our Democracy[72] and Is Donald Trump the Master of BS?[73]—to name a few.

Ed Schultz, who hosts News with Ed Schultz, also routinely ran segments that criticized Trump. "Who's gonna stop Donald Trump!?"[74] pleaded Schultz before a segment on how the GOP was worried about the reality-TV star's unstoppable rise. Schultz also aired an interview[75] with Bernie Sanders lambasting Trump's bigotry and sexism and calling Clinton "far and away the superior candidate." ...

Lesser-known names on RT America have also criticized Trump on-air. Lee Camp, who hosts the satirical show Redacted Tonight, has mocked Trump relentlessly, calling one segment on climate change Why Donald Trump Is Dangerous For All Humanity.[76] ...

A simple look through RT America's YouTube channel throws up numerous clips in which guests refer to Trump as misogynistic, bigoted, and racist. Guests on RT America have also claimed Trump does not stand up for regular workers[77], that his presidency would be exceedingly harmful to the markets[78], that he is not to be trusted on Social Security[79], and that his election could be more threatening to the global economy than ISIS[80]. A political psychologist invited on to discuss whether Trump was a "textbook narcissist" called Trump "unstable."[81] ...

RT America has also critically covered Trump's plans to "load up Guantánamo" with "bad dudes,"[82] run negative segments on his personal taxes[83], reported on Latinos fearing deportation[84] of friends and family, criticized his joke[85] about assassinating Hillary Clinton, covered controversy around his choice of Steve Bannon[86] as chief strategist, and ran segments calling both his health-care[87] and foreign-policy[88] plans lacking in detail.

From *The New Intelligence Report On Russia*[89]:

The report contains not a shred of forensic evidence that the Russian government directed the hacks of the DNC or of John Podesta ...

Instead of demonstrating conclusive links between the government of Russia and the hackers or between the government of Russia and Wikileaks, we are provided with a series of undocumented, evidence-free assertions of "high confidence" that Vladimir Putin directed an influence campaign to discredit Hillary Clinton in order to hurt her chances at the polls in November.

The report is marred by a reliance on innuendo and amateur psychological insights into Putin's motives, while adding no new forensic or other hard evidence. Nowhere does the report indicate that ODNI's sweeping conclusions were based on either HUMINT (human intelligence) or SIGINT (signals intelligence).

From *Russiagate Is More Fiction Than Fact*[90]:

Within 24 hours of Clinton's concession speech, top officials gathered "to engineer the case that the election wasn't entirely on the up-and-up.... Already, Russian hacking was the centerpiece of the argument."

RT preferred Bernie to Hillary, but when Bernie accepted the primaries defeat and endorsed Hillary, RT broadcasted his support to Hillary, and they aided Hillary against Trump in other ways. Videos posted on the RT Facebook page include Ed Schultz delivering Bernie Sanders' endorsement of Hillary Clinton[91] and Hillary speaking at a rally in Philadelphia[92].

Hillary's energy policies benefited Russia. The suppression of U.S. natural gas production and anti-fracking under environmental pretexts was a mainstream policy of the Democratic Party since 2013. Democrats made Massachusetts depend on Russia for natural gas, despite being just a few hundred miles from the Marcellus Shale, one of the world's largest natural gas fields[93]. Even the Assessment recognized that anti-fracking propaganda was reflective of the interests of Russian Federation (p. 8):

RT runs anti-fracking programming, highlighting environmental issues and the impacts on public health. This is likely reflective of the Russian Government's concern about the impact of fracking and US natural gas production on the global energy market and the potential challenges to Gazprom's profitability (5 October).

Of course, the MSM has misreported the Assessment. A broad assault on the energy industry – to *"disrupt Florida and other U.S. energy pipelines*" and to "*disrupt the booming American energy industry*" – has been conducted by Obama, Hillary, and the Democratic Party since 2010. A "Russian connection" has been acknowledged by some MSM outlets only later, like in *In Russian trolls' post-election task: Disrupt Florida and other U.S. energy pipelines* (McClatchy DC, May 2018)[94]

A television crew from Russia's largest state-backed network swooped into downtown Miami two days before New Year's Eve, 2016, on a curious mission. RT, the network formerly known as Russia Today, was there to provide global news coverage of one of five unremarkable rallies across Florida that day aimed at turning the public against the nearly completed, $3 billion Sabal Trail Pipeline designed to carry natural gas to the state from Alabama.

Climate of Fear in Cyber-Security

From Dec. 30, 2016 – Jan. 2, 2017, Mark Maunder, CEO of the security company Wordfence, was among many vocal critics of the wrong and incompetent FBI-DHS report *GRIZZLY STEPPE*. A month and a half later, he was afraid to criticize the new version of the same report, citing the *political nature of this issue*, apparently because he feared the repercussions of such criticisms. Most likely, the danger was coming from Big Tech, including the *Masters of the Universe*, which were triggered by the travel ban[95] and joined "the Resistance". They immediately developed zero tolerance for anybody and anything not opposing President Trump.

In a Dec. 30, 2016 post *US Govt Data Shows 'Russia' Used Outdated Ukrainian PHP Malware*[96], Mark Maunder even insisted that *Russia* be put in quotes. In a Jan. 2, 2017 post[97], Mark Maunder confirmed the results he had published. He and two other security researchers from Wordfence analyzed and compared data from the *GRIZZLY STEPPE* report to the real world. They concluded:

On Friday we published an analysis of the FBI and DHS Grizzly Steppe report. The report was widely seen as proof that Russian intelligence operatives hacked the US 2016 election. ***We showed that the PHP malware in the report is old, freely available from a Ukrainian hacker group*** *and is an administrative tool for hackers. We also performed an analysis on the IP addresses included in the report and showed that they originate from 61 countries and 389 different organizations with no clear attribution to Russia.*

The post also quoted the opinions of Jeffrey Carr[98] (founder of the *Suits and Spooks* conference and a lecturer at the Army War College and the Defense Intelligence Agency) and Robert M. Lee[99] (CEO and founder of the security company Dragos) who independently analyzed the same report and arrived at similar conclusions. The post also referenced general media articles, sometimes quoting the same researchers: *White House fails to make case that Russian hackers tampered with election*[100] (Ars Technica) and *Grizzly Misstep: Security Experts Call Russia Hacking*

Report "Poorly Done," and *"Fatally Flawed"*[101] (Fortune.com).

But his Feb. 13, 2017 post[102] about *Enhanced Grizzly Steppe Report* entirely avoided criticizing its data or methodology. Why? Mark Maunder practically acknowledged intimidation:

Final note regarding comments: Please note that due to the political nature of this issue, we won't be publishing any comments with political overtones. Our focus is simply on the data that DHS released and the data we are seeing ourselves and our analysis of it. Thank you.

Many cyber-security companies are forced to use **doublespeak**, similar to that of many climate related research papers in the first decade of this century.

(**Warning**: the following few paragraphs are boring.) For example, a ESET Sednit paper[103], dated October 2016, starts with and uses a definition, consistent with that of CrowdStrike and the DNC:

The Sednit group — also known as APT28, Fancy Bear and Sofacy — is a group of attackers operating since 2004 if not earlier and whose main objective is to steal confidential information from specific targets.

Only in one place does it acknowledge that neither the narrative nor the definition is true:

As security researchers, what we call "the Sednit group" is merely a set of software and the related network infrastructure, which we can hardly correlate with any specific organization.

A 2018 paper *LOJAX First UEFI rootkit found in the wild, courtesy of the Sednit group*[104] shows the same contradiction. It even refers to authorities blaming Sednit for multiple security breaches:

Sednit also known as APT28, Sofacy, Strontium and Fancy Bear – has been operating since at least 2004, and has made headlines frequently in the past years: it is believed to be behind major, high profile attacks. For instance, several security companies as well as the US Department of Justice named the group as being responsible for the Democratic National Committee (DNC) hack just before the US 2016 elections. The group is also presumed to be behind the hacking of global television network TV5Monde, the World Anti-Doping Agency (WADA) email leak and many others.

Only in one place does it acknowledge that the Sednit group is not a group of people but a software and network infrastructure:

What we call 'the Sednit group' is merely a set of software and the related network infrastructure, which we can hardly correlate authoritatively with any specific organization.

Congressional investigations did not look at these issues. The House Intelligence Committee has not asked independent network security experts. From *Fix Is In:*

*House Committee on 'Russian Hacking' Includes Only DNC-Hired Tech Experts (*Breitbart, Mar 7, 2017*)*[105]:

A list of witnesses scheduled to appear at a House Permanent Select Committee on Intelligence Open Hearing on 'Russian Active Measures' contains a glaring problem: the only technical experts scheduled to testify are from CrowdStrike. CrowdStrike is a firm hired by the Democratic National Committee (DNC) and has become the primary source of the narrative about 'Russian hacking' of the 2016 election and has acted as a mouthpiece for the Democrats since last June."

Even then, CrowdStrike refused to testify before the Committee; its officers provided some input behind the scene, but not under oath or penalty of perjury, and without cross-examination.

Final Remarks

This book became possible thanks to using the Honest Search Engine at https://defyccc.com/hs

See https://defyccc.com/TheMuellerReport for endnotes, links, supplementary material, and errata. That page also allows you to report errors and ask questions.

If you enjoyed reading this book, please post a review and recommend it to a friend!

Appendix ROBERT MUELLER: UNMASKED, by Louie Gohmert (R-TX)

Excerpts and Comments[106]

"Robert Mueller has a long and sordid history of illicitly targeting innocent people that is a stain upon the legacy of American jurisprudence."

"In his early years as FBI Director, most Republican members of Congress gave Mueller a pass in oversight hearings, allowing him to avoid tough questions. After all, we were continually told, "Bush appointed him." I gave him easy questions the first time I questioned him in 2005 out of deference to his Vietnam service. Yet, the longer I was in Congress, the more conspicuous the problems became. As I have said before of another Vietnam veteran [McCain?], just because someone deserves our respect for service or our sympathy for things that happened to them in the military, that does not give them the right to harm our country later. As glaring problems came to light, I toughened up my questions in the oversight hearings."

"CONGRESSMAN CURT WELDON DEFEATED BY MUELLER'S FBI

During my first term in Congress, 2005-2006, Congressman Curt Weldon delivered some powerful and relentless allegations about the FBI having prior knowledge that 9-11 was coming. ... Understand, I am not a 9-11 denier, nor a big conspiracy advocate. I am simply relaying things for which Congressman Weldon lambasted people at the top of the FBI and other places. ... In 2006, the Robert Mueller-led FBI took horrendously unjust actions to derail Curt Weldon's re-election bid just weeks before the vote... Please understand what former FBI officials have told me: the FBI would NEVER go after a member of Congress, House or Senate, without the full disclosure to and blessing of the FBI Director. ... **The early morning raid by Mueller's FBI with all the media outside, obviously alerted by the FBI, had achieved its goal of colluding to abuse the federal justice system to silence Curt Weldon** by ending his political career. Mueller's FBI worked it like a charm. If the Clintons and Berger manipulated Weldon's reelection to assure his defeat, they did it with the artful aid of Mueller, all while George W. Bush was President. Is any of this sounding familiar?"

This was written months before a similar pre-dawn FBI raid against Roger Stone, ordered by Mueller as the Special Counsel.

"People say those kinds of things just don't happen in America. They certainly seemed to when Mueller was in charge of the FBI and they certainly seem to while he is Special Counsel, as well. It appears clear that President Obama and his myrmidons knew of Mueller's reputation, that he could be used to take out their political opponents should such extra-legal actions become politically necessary. To the great dismay of the many good, decent and straight arrow FBI agents, Obama begged Mueller to stay on for two more years than the 10 years the law allowed. Obama then asked Congress to approve Mueller's waiver allowing him to stay on two extra years.

Perhaps the leaders in Congress did not realize what they were doing in approving it. I did. It was a major mistake, and I said so at the time. This is also why I objected strenuously the moment I heard Deputy Attorney General Rod Rosenstein appointed his old friend Bob Mueller to be Special Counsel to go after President Trump.

I was one of the few who were NOT surprised when Mueller started selecting his assistants in the Special Counsel's office who had reputations for being bullies, for indicting people who were not guilty of the charges, for forcing people toward bankruptcy by running up their attorney's fees (while the bullies in the Special Counsel's office enjoy an apparently endless government budget), or by threatening innocent family members with prosecution so the Special Counsel's victim would agree to pleading guilty to anything to prevent the Kafka-esque prosecutors from doing more harm to their families."

"MUELLER'S ILLEGAL RAID ON CONGRESSIONAL OFFICES

There is a doctrine in our experiment in self-government mandating that all parts of the government must have oversight to prevent power from corrupting and absolute power from corrupting absolutely. The Congress and Senate are accountable to the voters as is the President. All the massive bloated bureaucracy is supposed to be accountable to the Congress. ...

As I learned from talking with attorneys who had helped the House previously with this issue, if the FBI or another law enforcement entity needed to search something on the House side of the Capitol or House office buildings, they contacted the House Counsel, whether with a warrant or request. The House Counsel with approval of the Speaker, would go through the Congress Members documents, computers, flash drives, or anything that might have any bearing on what was being sought as part of the investigation. They would honestly determine what was relevant and what was not, and what was both irrelevant and privileged from Executive Branch review. Normally, if there were a dispute or question, it could be presented to a federal judge for a private in-chamber review to determine if it were privileged or relevant. If the DOJ or FBI were to get a warrant and gather all computers or documents in a Congressman's office without the recovered items being screened to insure they are not privileged from DOJ seizure, the DOJ would be risking that an entire case might be thrown out because of things improperly recovered and "fruit of the poisonous tree," preventing the use of even things that were not privileged. However, FBI Director Mueller seemed determined to throw over 200 years of Constitutional restraints to the wind so he could let Congress know he was the unstoppable government bully who could potentially waltz into our offices whenever he wished. In the case of Congressman William Jefferson, Democrat of Louisiana, Mueller was willing to risk a reversal of a slam dunk criminal case just to send a message to the rest of Congress: you don't mess with the Zohan, if the Zohan is Bob Mueller.

That Congressman Jefferson was guilty of something did not surprise most observers when, amidst swirling allegations, $90,000 in cold hard cash was found in his freezer. As we understood it, the FBI had a witness who was wired and basically got Jefferson on tape taking money. They had mountains of indisputable evidence to prove their case. They had gotten an entirely appropriate warrant to search his home and had even more mountains of evidence to nail the lid on his coffin, figuratively speaking.

The FBI certainly did not need to conduct an unsupervised search of a Congressman's office to put their unbeatable case at risk. Apparently, the risk was worth it to Mueller so he could show the Members of Congress who could harass or destroy them whenever he wished. Apparently, the FBI knew just the right federal judge who would disregard the Constitution and allow Mueller's minions to do their dirty work."

*** As the FBI director, Mueller apparently subscribed to the philosophy that the FBI is above Congress and other executive agencies, much like the NKVD and KGB were in the Soviet Union in 1934-56. Even the Soviet Communists decided to abolish this practice. The last practitioner, Lavrentiy Beria, was executed by a firing squad in 1956.

Democrats have been criminalizing political debates and using the DOJ, the FBI, and the IRS to silence their opponents since Obama's first term. Each actual prosecution silenced a large number of conservatives, who didn't want to become the next victim. Some Republicans were complicit in that passively or even actively. ***

"THE WITCH HUNT AGAINST REPUBLICAN SENATOR TED STEVENS AND HIS TRAGIC DEATH

Ted Stevens had served in the U.S. Senate since 1968 and was indicted in 2008 by the U.S. Justice Department. One would think before the U.S. government would seek to destroy a sitting U.S. Senator, there would be no question whatsoever of his guilt. One would be completely wrong in thinking so when the FBI Director is Robert Mueller.

Roll Call provides us with General Colin Powell's take on Ted Stevens: "According to former Secretary of State Colin Powell, who had worked closely with the senator since his days as President Ronald Reagan's national security adviser, the senator was 'a trusted individual ... someone whose word you could rely on. I never heard in all of those years a single dissenting voice with respect to his integrity, with respect to his forthrightness, and with respect to the fact that when you shook hands with Ted Stevens, or made a deal with Ted Stevens, it was going to be a deal that benefited the nation in the long run, one that he would stick with."

Such a glowing reputation certainly did not inhibit Mueller's FBI from putting Stevens in its cross-hairs, pushing to get an indictment that came 100 days before his election, and engaging in third world dictator-type tactics to help an innocent man lose his election, after which he lost his life. As reported by NPR, after the conviction and the truth came rolling out about the framing and conviction of Senator Stevens, the new Attorney General Eric Holder, had no choice. He "abandoned the Stevens case in April 2009 after uncovering new and 'disturbing' details about the prosecution..." Unfortunately for Ted Stevens, his conviction came only eight days before his election, which tipped the scales on a close election. ...

Does this sound familiar yet? The allegation was that Senator Stevens had not paid the full amount for improvements to his Alaska cabin. As *Roll Call* reported, he had actually overpaid for the improvements by over twenty percent. *Roll Call* went on to state: "But relying on false records and fueled by testimony from a richly rewarded 'cooperating' witness... government prosecutors convinced jurors to find him guilty just eight days before the general election which he lost by less than 2 percent of the vote."

Director Mueller either did control or could have controlled what happened to the lead FBI agent that destroyed a well-respected U.S. Senator. That U.S. Senator was not only completely innocent of the manufactured case against him, he was an honest and honorable man. Under Director Mueller's overriding supervision, the wrongdoer who helped manufacture the case stayed on and the whistleblower was punished. Obviously, the FBI Director wanted his FBI agents to understand that honesty would be punished if it revealed wrongdoing within Mueller's organization.

Further, not only was evidentiary proof of Senator Stevens' innocence concealed from the Senator's defense attorneys by the FBI, there was also a witness that provided compelling testimony that Stevens' had done everything appropriately. That witness, however, was sent back to Alaska by FBI agents, unbeknownst to the Senator's defense attorneys.

This key exonerating testimony was placed out of reach for Senator Stevens' defense. Someone should have gone to jail for this illegality within the nation's top law enforcement agency. Instead, Senator Stevens lost his seat, and surprise, surprise, Mueller's FBI helped another elected Republican bite the dust. Unfortunately, I am not speaking figuratively.

In August of 2010, former Senator Stevens boarded his doomed plane. But for the heinous, twisted and corrupt investigation by the FBI, and inappropriate prosecution by the DOJ, he would have still been a sitting U.S. Senator. Don't forget, one vote in the Senate was critical to ObamaCare becoming law also. If Senator Stevens was still there, it would not have become law."

The millions of families that lost their insurance because of ObamaCare can thank Robert Mueller for that. Mueller's prosecution method was to select a target and then to destroy it *by any means necessary*, especially by the abuse of the judicial process and his prosecutorial discretion. His favorite victims were businessmen and Republican lawmakers.

"THE FRAMING OF SCOOTER LIBBY

In 2003, during yet another fabricated and politically-charged FBI investigation, this one "searching" for the leak of CIA agent Valery Plame's identity to the media. Robert Mueller's very dear close friend James Comey was at the time serving as the Deputy Attorney General. Comey convinced then Attorney General John Ashcroft that he should recuse himself from the Plame investigation. At the time, Ashcroft was in the hospital.

After Deputy A.G. Comey was successful in securing Ashcroft's recusal, Comey then got to choose the Special Counsel. [Under a different statute than the current Special Counsel] He then looked about for someone who was completely independent of any relationships that might affect his independence and settled upon his own child's godfather and named Patrick Fitzgerald to investigate the source of the leak. So much for the independence of the Special Counsel.

The entire episode was further revealed as a fraud when it was later made public that Special Prosecutor Fitzgerald, FBI Director Mueller, and Deputy Attorney Comey had very early on learned that the source of Plame's identity leak came from Richard Armitage. But neither Comey nor Mueller nor Fitzgerald wanted Armitage's scalp. Oh no. These so-called apolitical, fair-minded pursuers of their own brand of justice were after a bigger name in the Bush administration like Vice

President Dick Cheney or Karl Rove. Yet they knew from the beginning that these two men were not guilty of anything.

Nonetheless, **Fitzgerald, Mueller and Comey pursued Cheney's chief of staff, Scooter Libby, as a path to ensnare the Vice President.** According to multiple reports, Fitzgerald had twice offered to drop all charges against Libby if he would 'deliver' Cheney to him. There was nothing to deliver.

Is any of this sounding familiar?"

Acknowledgments

Thanks to A.P. and other individuals without whom this book would have been impossible.

About the Author

Leo Goldstein has a unique background for somebody writing about elections, Washington corruption, and national politics. His experience is in computer software and networks, with a large chunk of it related to cyber security. He also has a M.Sc. in Mathematics from Lomonosov Moscow State University. He knows a thing or two about capabilities of white hat and black hat hackers from Russia and Eastern Europe and doesn't fall for the stories that Russia hacked the DNC.

This book became possible because the author lives in Texas, and he doesn't depend on Silicon Valley's *Masters of the Universe*.

Endnotes and References

[1] https://www.foxnews.com/politics/trump-facing-coup-fbi-brass-was-in-cahoots-dowd-tells-foxs-kilmeade For convenience of the paperback readers, endnotes and links are also listed on https://defyccc.com/TheMuellerReport

[2] https://www.nationalreview.com/2018/09/trump-russia-probe-robert-mueller-investigation/, https://www.nationalreview.com/2018/03/second-special-counsel-fisa-not-necessary/

[3] Rod Rosenstein's memo from May 2017, appointing Robert Mueller as a Special Counsel:
https://www.justice.gov/opa/press-release/file/967231/download

[4] Read Peter Schweizer's book **Clinton Cash**, or download *From Russia with Money*:
http://www.g-a-i.org/wp-content/uploads/2016/08/Report-Skolkvovo-08012016.pdf

[5] http://excessofdemocracy.com/blog/2013/7/ranking-the-most-liberal-and-conservative-law-firms

[6]
https://www.opensecrets.org/orgs/recips.php?id=D000022322&cycle=2016; the Open Secrets and excessofdemocracy.com used different methodologies.

[7] https://archive.is/Wgabw , https://archive.is/2v8fG

[8] They might have second thoughts about that now:
https://archive.fo/5fjCA

[9] https://www.wilmerhale.com/en/solutions/international-trade-investment-and-market-access

[10] https://www.wilmerhale.com/en/contact-us/beijing

[11] https://www.wilmerhale.com/en/solutions/international-trade-investment-and-market-access/china-trade

[12] https://www.wilmerhale.com/en/about

[13] https://www.wilmerhale.com/en/solutions/international-trade-investment-and-market-access

[14] https://www.conservapedia.com/Gender_identity_disorder, https://www.britannica.com/science/gender-dysphoria

[15] https://www.wilmerhale.com/en/about/public-service-and-pro-bono

[16] https://www.wilmerhale.com/en/about/alumni%20network

[17] https://www.foxnews.com/politics/top-mueller-investigators-democratic-ties-raise-new-bias-questions,

https://www.wired.com/story/robert-mueller-special-counsel-investigation-team

[18] https://www.forbes.com/sites/cdw/2017/09/21/the-next-grave-threat-cybersecurity

[19] https://fedtechmagazine.com/article/2017/03/former-fbi-director-cybersecurity-tough-questions-must-come-top

[20] https://www.foxnews.com/opinion/was-fridays-declassified-report-claiming-russian-hacking-of-the-2016-election-rigged

[21] https://www.youtube.com/watch?v=mEzqHB7QgLMt=1510 -- I hope Google YouTube did not delete this video by the time you are reading this, as it has done to shorter and more popular clips of that interview.

[22] Curiously, both Trump and his enemies wanted Comey to be fired.

[23] https://www.businesswire.com/news/home/20170119005600/en/China-Oceanwide-IDG-Capital-Announce-Agreement-Acquire

[24] Mueller's disclosure is available at https://www.politico.com/f/?id=0000015d-c404-d494-a77f-e6163c3a0001

[25] https://archive.is/b7v0Z

[26] Mueller is listed as a speaker at https://cdwevents.cio.com/ehome/cdw/speakers/

[27] http://chinaoceanwideusa.com

[28] https://www.prnewswire.com/news-releases/china-oceanwide-completes-acquisition-of-idg-300431673.html

[29] https://defyccc.com/masters-of-the-universe-ban-alex-jones-and-infowars

[30] https://archive.is/JF9ta

[31] https://www.infowars.com/update-youtube-bans-alex-jones-channel

[32] https://www.justice.gov/file/1035477/download

[33] No, it's not a joke. "U.S. Special Counsel Robert Mueller's office said on Wednesday that **self-proclaimed hackers in Russia stole evidence in an attempt to tarnish its investigation** of a firm charged with funding a Russian propaganda campaign to interfere in the 2016 U.S. election …" – Reuters, January 31, 2019, https://archive.is/YLaVd

[34] https://defyccc.com/censorship-by-motu-is-alive-and-well, https://defyccc.com/twitter-shadowbanning, https://defyccc.com/twitter-labeled-trump-supporters-russian-bots/

[35] Mueller's disclosure is available at https://www.politico.com/f/?id=0000015d-c404-d494-a77f-e6163c3a0001.

[36] CHRISTOPHER PAINTER: I called Shawn Henry who just recently retired who happened to be in an executive retreat with Director Mueller who was having dinner with him and he said, "Hey, this happening." http://www.atlanticcouncil.org/?id=10323:building-a-secure-cyber-future-transcript-5-23-12

[37] https://wattsupwiththat.com/2018/07/13/dangerous-pseudo-science-in-cyber-security

[38] http://dailycaller.com/2017/03/07/house-intel-chair-announces-open-hearing-on-russia-probe

[39] http://archive.is/x4xoz

[40] https://sk.ru/foundation/nuclear/p/goals.aspx

[41] https://sk.ru/foundation/space/p/goals.aspx

[42] https://archive.fo/GaA1R

[43] https://archive.fo/MoszC

[44] See VisionLabs, for example. https://archive.fo/84qA1

[45] https://www.nationalreview.com/2018/03/clinton-russia-collusion-evidence/

[46] https://www.nationalreview.com/2017/04/clinton-russia-ties-bill-hillary-sold-out-us-interests-putin-regime/

[47] https://www.youtube.com/watch?v=AKoCwHGJ1To - this YouTube video clip of that interview is another survivor of Google purges, and I can only hope it is available when you read it. A more popular version, embedded in the NR article, was deleted.

[48] European lawyer Alex van der Zwaan is an exception. He is not connected to Trump and doesn't reside in Russia.

[49] https://www.hannity.com/wp-content/uploads/2018/04/Gohmert_Mueller_UNMASKED.pdf

[50] https://www.dailymail.co.uk/news/article-4034038/Ex-British-ambassador-WikiLeaks-operative-claims-Russia-did-NOT-provide-Clinton-emails-handed-D-C-park-intermediary-disgusted-Democratic-insiders.html

[51] https://archive.vn/Nc7n2

[52] https://archive.vn/d3QBU

[53] https://defyccc.com/ica_text_brennan_clapper_activities

[54] https://www.foxnews.com/opinion/more-indications-intel-assessment-of-russian-interference-in-election-was-rigged

[55] https://defyccc.com/crowdstrike-crooked-and-shrill

[56] https://climateaudit.org/2017/10/02/guccifer-2-from-january-to-may-2016/#comment-775518

[57] https://defyccc.com/crowdstrike-mis-department-and-the-dnc

[58] https://defyccc.com/silicon-valley-totalitarian-dystopia

[59] https://www.us-cert.gov/sites/default/files/publications/JAR_16-20296A_GRIZZLY STEPPE-2016-1229.pdf

[60] https://www.thedailybeast.com/how-the-us-hobbled-its-hacking-case-against-russia-and-enabled-truthers;
Robert M. Lee was quoted from http://www.robertmlee.org/critiques-of-the-dhsfbis-grizzly-steppe-report.

[61] https://www.usatoday.com/story/tech/news/2017/11/01/russians-used-facebook-way-other-advertisers-do-tapping-into-its-data-mining-machine/817826001/

[62] https://archive.is/Cns71

[63] https://web.archive.org/web/20171010100423/https:/www.us

atoday.com/story/opinion/2017/10/03/readers-sound-off-no-one-pays-attention-facebook-ads-anyway/728895001/

[64] https://newsroom.fb.com/news/2017/09/information-operations-update/

[65] https://www.usatoday.com/story/news/2018/05/11/what-we-found-facebook-ads-russians-accused-election-meddling/602319002

[66] https://www.thenation.com/article/rt-america-was-not-pro-trump/

[67] https://www.youtube.com/watch?v=X-edBT-1Sec

[68] https://www.rt.com/shows/big-picture/368650-trump-free-speech-us/

[69] https://www.rt.com/shows/big-picture/367484-trunp-cabinet-positions-politicians/

[70] https://www.rt.com/shows/big-picture/372128-trump-crash-economic-us/

[71] https://www.rt.com/shows/big-picture/370918-trump-internet-election-future/

[72] https://www.rt.com/shows/big-picture/370485-trump-oil-/

[73] https://www.rt.com/shows/big-picture/369583-obamacare-trump-us-army/

[74] https://www.youtube.com/watch?v=9ZZUcUqYLpU

[75] https://www.youtube.com/watch?v=hQFnaDUaRkU

[76] https://www.youtube.com/watch?v=7GYs_0I4s64

[77] https://www.youtube.com/watch?v=D0e3KV6zTqk

[78] https://www.youtube.com/watch?v=acT-H4c3zBo

[79] https://www.youtube.com/watch?v=vrbpi9pbM8477

[80] https://www.youtube.com/watch?v=WbE3vBsvocM

[81] https://www.youtube.com/watch?v=QXMEsYqsJlE

[82] https://www.youtube.com/watch?v=q1%E2%80%940dk5awl

[83] https://www.youtube.com/watch?v=xoeE5jXOflE

[84] https://www.youtube.com/watch?v=5mhh4fPZhGQ

[85] https://www.youtube.com/watch?v=QBEMPu0RCyM

[86] https://www.youtube.com/watch?v=cNC4lB_O12Q

[87] https://www.youtube.com/watch?v=0mRnLvFo9sk

[88] https://www.youtube.com/watch?v=04yGR0JZxWg

[89] https://www.thenation.com/article/the-new-intelligence-report-on-russia-shows-we-need-an-independent-bipartisan-commission-now-more-than-ever/

[90] https://www.thenation.com/article/russiagate-is-more-fiction-than-fact/

[91] https://www.facebook.com/RTAmerica/videos/10153626420741366/

[92] https://www.facebook.com/RTAmerica/videos/10153703175376366/

[93] https://defyccc.com/climate-alarmism-kills

[94] https://archive.is/zuPzh

[95] https://defyccc.com/when-silicon-valley-went-off-the-cliff

[96] https://www.wordfence.com/blog/2016/12/russia-malware-ip-hack/

[97] https://www.wordfence.com/blog/2017/01/election-hack-faq/

[98] https://medium.com/@jeffreycarr/fbi-dhs-joint-analysis-report-a-fatally-flawed-effort-b6a98fafe2fa

[99] http://www.robertmlee.org/critiques-of-the-dhsfbis-grizzly-steppe-report/

[100] http://arstechnica.com/security/2016/12/did-russia-tamper-with-the-2016-election-bitter-debate-likely-to-rage-on/

[101] http://fortune.com/2016/12/31/russian-hacking-grizzly-steppe/

[102] https://www.wordfence.com/blog/2017/02/russia-election-hack-worpress-used/

[103] https://www.welivesecurity.com/wp-content/uploads/2016/10/eset-sednit-part1.pdf

[104] https://cdn1.esetstatic.com/ESET/US/resources/datasheets/ESETus-datasheet-lojax.pdf

[105] https://www.breitbart.com/politics/2017/03/09/house-committee-russian-hacking-includes-only-dnc-hired-tech-experts

[106] https://gohmert.house.gov/news/documentsingle.aspx?DocumentID=398634

Made in the USA
Lexington, KY
29 March 2019